IMAGES
of America

FORT ONTARIO

GUARDIAN OF THE NORTH

The Daughters of the American Revolution placed this stone marker in front of the main gate at Fort Ontario in 1906. The stone reads as follows:

FORT ONTARIO
BUILT BY ENGLISH UNDER GOVERNOR SHIRLEY 1755
CAPTURED & DESTROYED BY FRENCH
UNDER MARQUIS OF MONTCALM 1756
REBUILT BY ENGLISH UNDER LORD AMHERST 1759
DESTROYED BY AMERICANS 1778*—REBUILT BY ENGLISH 1782
SURRENDERED BY ENGLISH & GARRISONED BY UNITED STATES 1796
CAPTURED & DESTROYED BY ENGLISH FLEET UNDER ADMIRAL YEO 1814
REBUILT OF EARTH & TIMBER BY UNITED STATES 1839–1842
REBUILT OF STONE & CONCRETE BY UNITED STATES 1863–1870
POST ENLARGED AND BUILT OF BRICK BY
UNITED STATES 1903–1905

THIS TABLET ERECTED BY THE
FORT OSWEGO CHAPTER
DAUGHTERS OF THE AMERICAN REVOLUTION
JULY 4, 1906

*Note: The date of 1778 is incorrect; it should be 1779.

IMAGES
of America

FORT ONTARIO
GUARDIAN OF THE NORTH

George A. and Carol Reed

ARCADIA
PUBLISHING

ISBN 978-0-7385-0284-7

Published by Arcadia Publishing
Charleston, South Carolina

Printed in the United States of America

Library of Congress Catalog Card Number: Applied for

For all general information contact Arcadia Publishing at:
Telephone 843-853-2070
Fax 843-853-0044
E-Mail sales@arcadiapublishing.com
For customer service and orders:
Toll-Free 1-888-313-2665

Visit us on the Internet at www.arcadiapublishing.com

On the cover: Troops stationed at Fort Ontario in 1899 stand by to fire the cannon.

This watercolor shows the second Fort Ontario as it looked in 1760. The artist painted it from the west side of the river, with the ruins of the earlier Fort Oswego in the foreground.

Contents

Introduction		7
1.	Wood Walls	9
2.	Stone and Wood	25
3.	Hospital	45
4.	Last Years as a Fortification	63
5.	World War II	73
6.	Safe Haven	81
7.	Historic Site	87
8.	Recent Years	111
Appendix		127

Introduction

A sign on the main gate claims that Fort Ontario was the oldest continuously garrisoned post in the U.S. Army. The fort shielded the northern border of the United States from 1755 until 1946.

The first Fort Ontario was built by the British in 1755. It was an eight-sided log structure, built on the bluff on the east side of the Oswego River. It had four buildings, a dry moat, and was armed with swivels, mortars, and cannons. French general Louis-Joseph Montcalm led 4,000 men in an attack on Oswego on August 14, 1756. Fort Ontario, two other forts, a small fleet of ships, and the hamlet of Oswego were destroyed.

The British used the site of Fort Ontario as a base for the attack on Fort Frontenac (Kingston). In 1759, they built a temporary fortification at the site of Fort Ontario. They defeated the attacking French troops, who lost the element of surprise. In August 1759, the British built a large five-bastioned fort, armed with 46 artillery pieces, near the site of the original Fort Ontario. The present historic site maintains this design. After the defeat of their French allies, the Indians continued fighting on the frontier. War broke out when they attacked British settlements on the frontier. Chief Pontiac led the war, which continued until July 31, 1766, when he made peace with Sir William Johnson under the guns of Fort Ontario.

During the American Revolution, the British held Fort Ontario and used it as a base for military operations against the New York colonists. In December 1777, British forces planned to isolate the New England colonies. The plan called for three British armies to come from three directions and meet in Albany. Lord William Howe was to advance up the Hudson River; Gen. John Burgoyne was to descend from Canada through Lake Champlain and Lake George; and Brig. Gen. Barry St. Leger was to travel eastward from Fort Ontario along the Mohawk River. St. Leger was stopped by an abortive siege at Fort Stanwix. On August 22, 1776, St. Leger and his men broke up their encampment. St. Leger retreated to Canada, taking Fort Ontario's garrison and artillery with him. Troops from Fort Stanwix burned Fort Ontario. In 1782, the British repaired and garrisoned Fort Ontario, which became a concern for Gen. George Washington. Washington ordered an attack on the fort, but the attack failed when American troops were seen by a woodcutting party from Fort Ontario. The fort remained in British hands for the next 13 years.

Two weeks after the American occupation of Fort Ontario, a civilian population started growing in Oswego. U.S. troops were removed from Fort Ontario after 1803. During this period, the fort fell into disrepair due to a shortage of money. British forces attacked Fort Ontario twice during the War of 1812. On June 20, 1813, they were repulsed by defenders at the fort. Their next attack, in May 1814, resulted in the destruction of the fort. During Pres. Martin Van Buren's administration, tension with Canada led to the construction of the third Fort Ontario. The main buildings were constructed between 1839 and 1844. The outer walls were built of wood and were painted white.

In the years between the "Patriot War" and the Civil War, Fort Ontario was typical of many small company-sized posts, across which the regular military was apportioned. During the Civil War, Fort Ontario saw no action but had two companies of soldiers stationed there. The fort was never completed. The last two buildings constructed in the old fort were the east and west guardhouses. The casemates were built but were not equipped with cannon. The exterior wall was left unfinished. After the Civil War ended, tensions with Great Britain continued on the northern frontier. Irish nationalists, the Fenians, began to conduct raids into Canada from the United States. Troops from Fort Ontario were dispatched by rail in an attempt to stop an Irish raid.

In 1894, troops from Fort Ontario were sent to Chicago to help quell riots during the Pullman Strike. With the advent of the Spanish American War, the garrison at Fort Ontario doubled to two companies. In 1899, 15 soldiers of the 9th U.S. Infantry at Fort Ontario were sent to the Philippine Islands during the Moro Insurrection. Fort Ontario was converted into a training installation. Between 1903 and 1905, the fort's outer works and dry moat were removed and a much enlarged military reservation was built. The fort had a garrison of between 300 and 400 men.

During World War I, a major hospital was operated at Fort Ontario. The fort was designated as General Hospital No. 5. Troops wounded during the war were shipped to New York City and then placed on special hospital trains that traveled to Oswego. In 1921, Fort Ontario once again became an infantry post. In 1933, the fort served as brigade headquarters. During World War II, the grounds encompassed 80 acres, with large shade trees and rows of new white barracks and older red brick homes, surrounding a broad green parade ground.

Between 1944 and 1946, Fort Ontario was used as an emergency center for 982 refugees fleeing from the Holocaust. This fort was the only wartime refugee shelter in the history of the United States. The center was run by the U.S. Department of Interior.

The end of World War II resulted in a severe housing shortage. Many soldiers took advantage of the GI Bill and attended Oswego State Teacher's College. The fort was used as veterans housing.

In 1949, Fort Ontario was transferred to the state of New York as a State Historic Site. The site was rebuilt to reflect a post-Civil War fort. In June 1962, a military detachment known as the Fort Ontario Guard was established. The unit now depicts a company of Civil War veterans. More than 10,000 people from all parts of the world visit Fort Ontario each year. It continues to serve as an inspiration and a memorial to all the troops who served and died at Fort Ontario.

The authors wish to thank the Fort Ontario staff for assisting in the preparation of this book and Bruce Frassinelli for his careful editing of the text.

One

Wood Walls

The first fort stood at the mouth of the Oswego River for 28 years before Fort Ontario was built. Called Fort Oswego, it was constructed in 1727 and was destroyed by the French in 1755. This painting depicts Fort Oswego *c.* 1749.

William Burnet, the governor of New York, realized the potential of the fur trade for the growth of the colony. He ordered the construction of "a stone house of strength" at Oswego near the trading center. In response, a two-story stone structure was built in 1727. Its U-shaped outer wall was held together by mud and clay, giving the fort a castlelike appearance. The outer walls were so weak that the commanding officer would not allow the fort's cannons to be fired,

for fear the wall would collapse. Commanded by a captain, between 10 and 20 soldiers of the Independent Companies were stationed at Fort Oswego from 1726 to 1755. In 1756, Fort Oswego was destroyed by the French. This view, looking north, depicts Fort Oswego *c.* 1755. Note the ships being constructed on the sandbar.

This early 20th-century illustration shows Fort Oswego as a log structure with a roof; contemporary French drawings do not include a roof. The fort was very small. The officer, a captain, had his quarters inside it, and the troops slept outside in log-and-bark huts.

The fur-trading village of Oswego contained between 20 and 64 log-and-bark structures to house traders. Fort Oswego was expanded in 1755, the year depicted in this painting; ships were being constructed there at that time. Note the sandbar in front of the fort.

Soldiers stationed at Fort Ontario from 1755 until 1756, represented here from left to right, were the Jersey Blues 51st Regiment of Foot, the 50th Regiment of Foot and the Independent Company. The Independent Company was relieved in 1755. After the fort was attacked by the French general Louis-Joseph Montcalm, the 50th and 51st Regiments ceased to be part of the British army. Fort Oswego is shown in the background of this painting.

In early times, the nation that ruled the mouth of the Oswego River dominated North America. Lakes, steams, and rivers were the earliest highways through the North American wilderness. Travel by land was difficult because of the thick virgin forest that enclosed the land. There were only two natural water routes into the interior of North America from the east coast: the St. Lawrence River and the Hudson-Mohawk-Oswego River valley. The St. Lawrence route had several disadvantages: a short season of navigation, floating ice, fog, and rapids. Oswego's route was longer but had an extended season and none of the St. Lawrence's other disadvantages. The convergence of the Oswego River and Lake Ontario was pivotal in the development of the Great Lakes region and of New York.

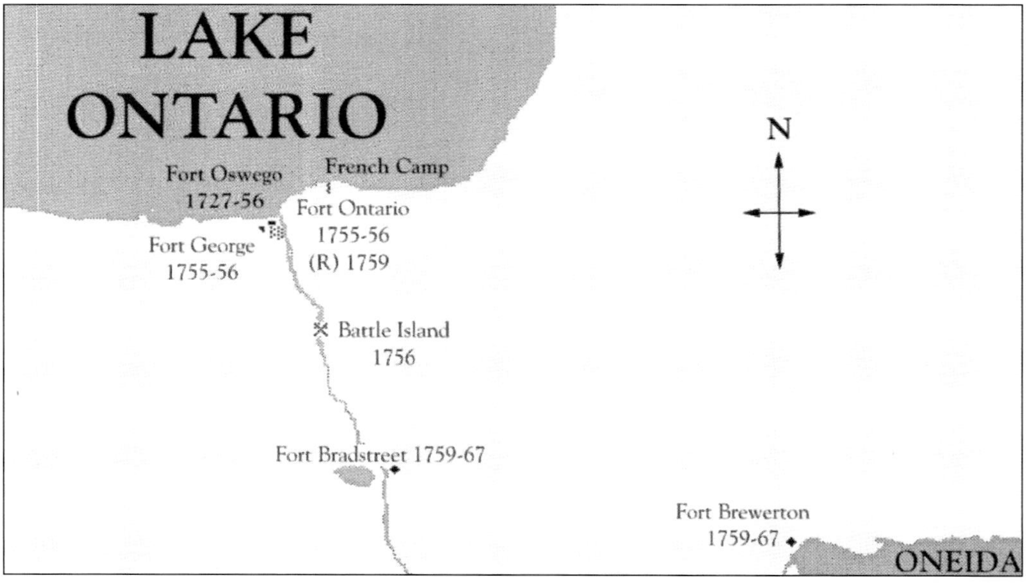

In the summer of 1755, the English sent Gen. William Shirley to Oswego to prepare an attack on Fort Niagara with Gen. Edward Braddock. Shirley had an eight-sided log structure built on the bluff on the east side of the Oswego River, a site previously recommended by Colonel von Romer. The structure was called Fort Ontario. It was a weak fort, designed to defend against Indian attack and built without consideration of a hill to the east that allowed an enemy to attack unobserved. It had four buildings but no blockhouse. Surrounded by a dry moat, the fort was armed with artillery, swivels, mortars, and cannons, and its walls were logs sharpened at the top. Plans called for a large central blockhouse and four small buildings, but these were never constructed.

The most strategic point for the supply of Oswego was the Great Carrying Place, known to the Native Americans as *De-O-Wain-Sta*. This 4-mile portage separated the Mohawk River from Wood Creek. The French governor ordered Capt. Gaspar Joseph Chaussegros de Lery to attack the Great Carrying Place. De Lery gathered 93 French officers, cadets, and soldiers, 166 Canadians, and 103 Indians at Fort de la Presentation, shown here. During two wintry weeks in March 1756, he and his troops marched through snow, fog, and ice to reach Fort Bull, built under the orders of the English general William Shirley. On March 27, they attacked the gate of the fort with axes. Before he took the fort, de Lery promised to spare all lives if the English surrendered. When his offer was greeted with ineffective bursts of grenades and musket fire, he and his men breached the gate with shouts of "Vive le Roi." They killed everyone they could lay hands on, including women and children; the wife of Lieutenant Bull was bayoneted by a Canadian soldier. After a magazine caught fire, they were forced to flee just before the fort exploded.

In August 1756, Fort Ontario was attacked and destroyed by French forces under the command of the Marquis de Montcalm. Montcalm, commander in chief of French forces in North America, gathered between 3,000 and 4,000 men at Fort Frontenac (Kingston) and then sailed down the eastern shore of Lake Ontario, traveling by night and camping by day. Upon arrival, Montcalm set up his infantry in a siege line one pistol shot from the walls of Fort Ontario. On August 10, 1756, the siege began. The English, who numbered 1,134, held out for three days. The fort was not built to withstand attack by heavy artillery. It was strong enough to hold out against 4-pound cannons, but Montcalm had 12-pound cannons. After Montcalm built a road and brought up his artillery, the English forces fired all their shell and ammunition, spiked their cannon, and abandoned the fort. They forded the Oswego River and joined the defenses at Fort Oswego. The French went on to take Fort Oswego and then Fort George on August 14, 1756. The English surrendered by raising the French flag. The French destroyed all three forts, the trading village, and the small fleet of ships. This view shows Fort Ontario from the Oswego River.

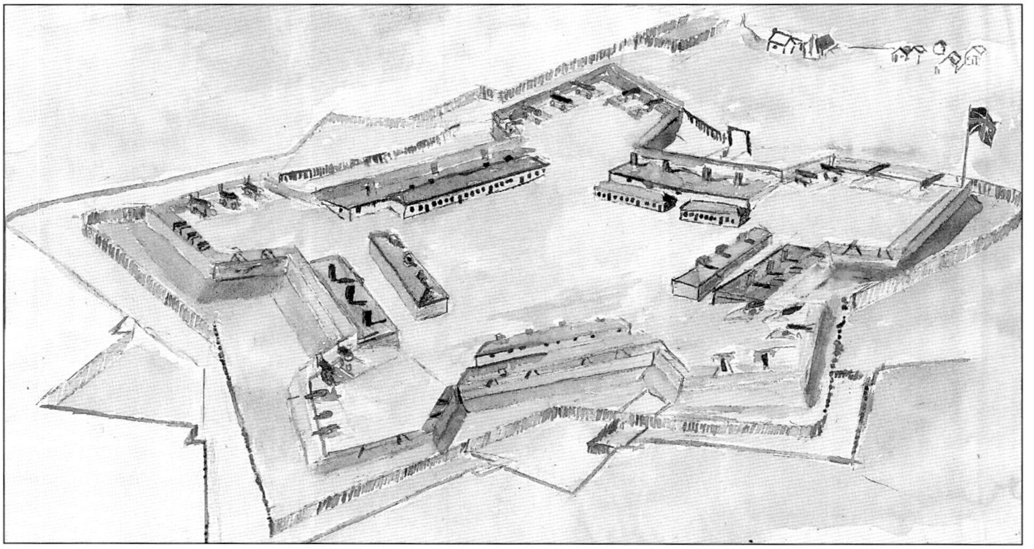

The first work on the second Fort Ontario began on August 17, 1759, three years after the Marquis de Montcalm's victory here. Gen. Thomas Gage launched the construction of a larger five-bastioned fort near the site of the original one. The new fort had extensive outer works, a dry moat, and emplacements for 46 artillery pieces. It was built to house a garrison of 500 men. The English intended to control the Great Lakes region.

The troops stationed at Fort Ontario in 1760 were the 55th Regiment of Foot. Their uniform was modified for the French and Indian War. Note the hats and coats cut back for frontier use. The eight-sided structure in the background of this painting is Fort Bradstreet, built in Fulton in 1759 to protect a vital portage and the supply route to Fort Ontario.

Troops stationed at Fort Ontario in 1777 were of the King's Royal Regiment of New York, the 8th Regiment of Foot, the 34th Regiment of Foot, and the Anspach Jaegers.

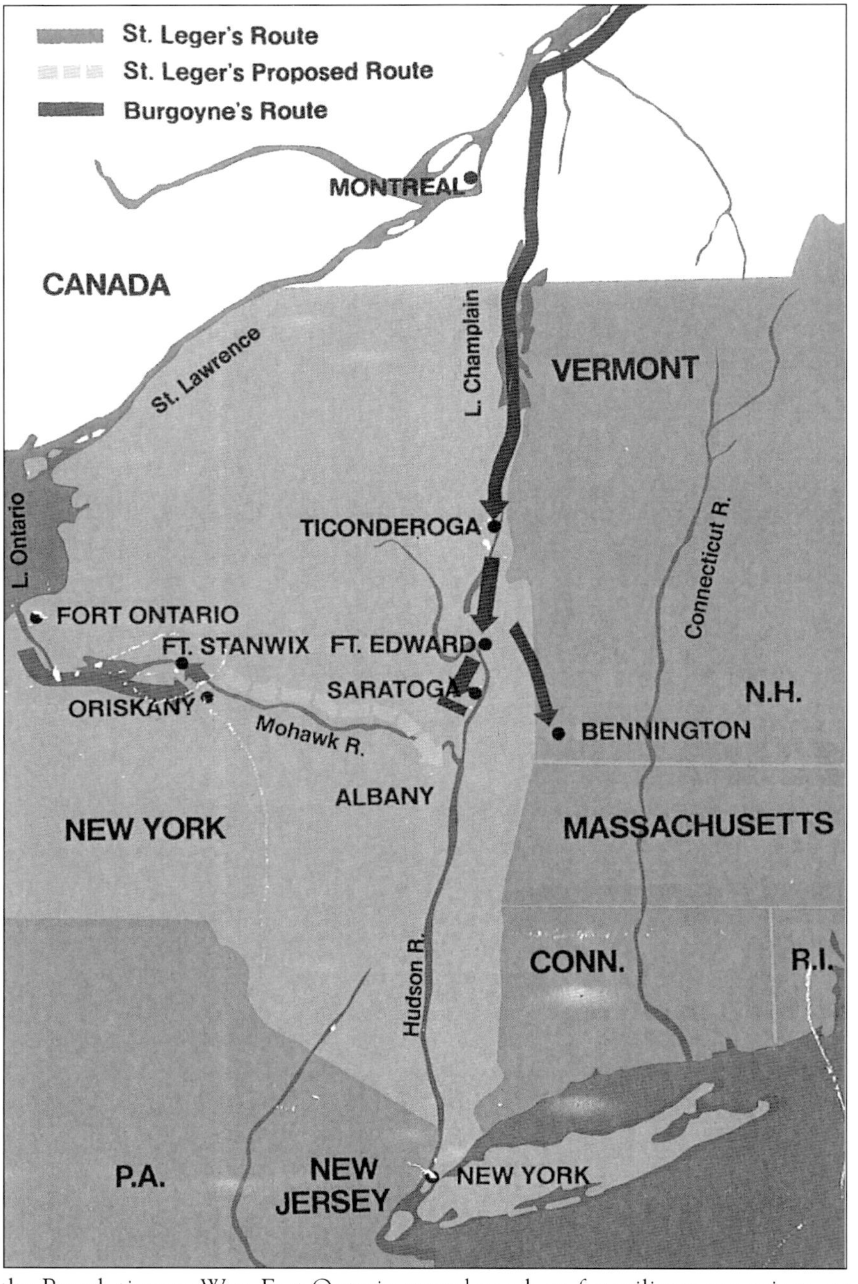

During the Revolutionary War, Fort Ontario served as a base for military operations against the New York colonists. In July 1777, Brig. Gen. Barry St. Leger used the fort as his base. At Fort Stanwix, he met solid resistance. Learning that an 800-man relief force was coming to the relief of Fort Stanwix, he set an ambush at Oriskany on August 6, 1777. While the English were engaged at Oriskany, troops in Fort Stanwix raided the British camp and seized the cannons, powder, and materials. On August 22, 1777, St. Leger and his troops broke camp and retreated in haste and confusion, leaving behind tents and a great part of their artillery. Four days later, they arrived at Fort Ontario, took the garrison and artillery from there, and retreated to Canada.

Fort Ontario remained without a regular garrison for some time after the retreat of Brig. Gen. Barry St. Leger. The Iroquois repeatedly requested that the garrison return to the fort. In July 1779, rebel troops from Fort Stanwix burned the buildings at Fort Ontario. The fort became a base for Loyalist-Iroquois raiding parties. In 1782, the British repaired and garrisoned Fort Ontario. The following winter, American forces tried and failed to take the fort in what became the last military expedition of the Revolutionary War. The British held Fort Ontario and all the other major northern posts for the 13 next years. This painting depicts Fort Ontario in 1789.

On November 19, 1794, American statesman John Jay obtained the British surrender of Fort Ontario and the other northern posts, which had been promised in the treaty of 1783. As a result, U.S. troops under Capt. James Bruff replaced Fort Ontario's last British garrison on July 14, 1796. In a letter to George Scriba dated July 15, 1796, Lt. Frederick Elmer described the event as follows: "I have the pleasure of informing you that the American flag, under a federal salute, was for the first time displayed from the citadel of this fort, at the hour of 10:00

this morning. A Captain (W.C.) Clark and Colonel (Robert) Fothergill were his Majesty's officers left with a detachment of 30 men for the protection of the works. From these gentlemen politeness and civility was displayed to us in adjusting the transfer. The buildings and gardens were left in the neatest order: and the latter being considerably extensive and in high culture, will be no small addition to the comfort of the American officers who succeed this summer." This view depicts Fort Ontario *c.* 1796.

During the War of 1812, Fort Ontario was attacked twice. On June 20, 1813, Maj. Gen. Gordon Drummond, the governor-general of Canada, and Commo. James Yeo attacked Fort Ontario. Yeo's ships made a sweep of the shoreline that included the burning of Sodus and a landing at Pultneyville. Yeo made three attempts to land troops and each time was repulsed by defenders at Fort Ontario. On May 5 and May 6, 1814, Drummond and Yeo returned with a force of seamen, marines, and soldiers who outnumbered the American soldiers, seamen, and militia by more than four to one. On the first day, they launched a naval bombardment followed by an abortive landing. They waited ten hours to attack and then were driven off. They continued shelling on the second day, waded ashore beneath a storm of cannon fire, and stormed the fort. This view represents Fort Ontario in 1814.

In the attack of May 6, 1814, the British charged the northwest rampart of the fort. U.S. Lt. Col. George Mitchell withdrew his militia and artillerists. A struggle took place inside the fort to prevent the British from lowering the American flag. Lt. John Hewett of the Royal Marines climbed to the top of the flagpole, tore down the large flag, and dragged it to the ground. Mitchell ordered his forces to retreat.

The British destroyed Fort Ontario, sacked the village, and scuttled the small fleet before leaving. American troops made no efforts to reconstruct Fort Ontario before the end of the War of 1812. Fort Ontario's earthworks remained, but all the buildings and the wooden stockade decayed and fell apart. As the defensive role of Fort Ontario changed, the village below its crumbling walls grew into a city.

Two

STONE AND WOOD

The third Fort Ontario was built between 1839 and 1844 as a direct reaction to tension along the border, caused by Canada's failed revolt for independence from England. U.S. troops were quartered temporarily in an Oswego hotel in July 1838, while engineers proceeded with the plans for a new fort. The walls were wooden revetments, painted white. The outer walls retained their 18th-century shape but were reinforced with timbers. Strengthened and manned, Fort Ontario served as a defense against an attack from the north when Britain and America were closer to the brink of war than has been generally realized.

In the years before the Civil War, Fort Ontario was typical of the many small company-sized posts. At the beginning of war, a garrison of regulars was stationed at the fort because the North had many reasons to believe that the British would support the South. Later, when that threat subsided, the garrison was reduced to one company and most of the cannons were shipped south for the war effort. Throughout the war, the fort served as a recruitment and induction center. It became a regional assembly point for volunteer units shortly after the attack on Fort Sumter. The only blood that was shed at Fort Ontario during the Civil War belonged to Capt. D.P. Hancock, who received a minor injury when a pistol accidentally discharged during a party being held in his honor. This early-20th-century photo shows Fort Ontario's dry moat and wooden walls. The stone walls were added in 1863.

During the draft riots of 1863, Fort Ontario served as a hiding place for federal records. Meanwhile, new construction to strengthen the fort continued. The wooden exterior walls were replaced by stone. Rifle and artillery casemates were built between 1863 and 1871. This photograph shows an artillery casemate that was never equipped with artillery.

During the summer of 1864, the 184th New York Volunteer Infantry was raised and inducted at Fort Ontario. The improvements and construction of casemates and stone walls was never completed. Congress cut off funds in 1877. This view shows the entrance to a rifle casemate and parts of the artillery casemates on the lower walls.

Fort Ontario had little defensive importance after the Civil War. It was maintained by Company F, 42nd Infantry, Veterans Reserve Corps, formerly called the Invalid Corps. This corps was comprised of soldiers who had been in combat and had either been wounded or were willing to reenlist for other than combat duty. This view shows Fort Ontario from the west side of Oswego Harbor. The wooden wall suggests that it was taken prior to 1877. The area below the fort was used to transport heavy guns to and from the fort. The Inner Harbor Lighthouse is on the left.

The enlisted men's quarters were built to house approximately 58 men. The troops lived on the second floor. For most of its 19th century history, Fort Ontario was garrisoned by one company of infantry or artillery with 45 to 70 men. When a second company was assigned to Fort Ontario, the men were housed in the attic. The ground floor housed the galley and a company room. The two small buildings at each corner were privies. Troops posing for this photograph were from Company F, Ware Reserve Corps, 1868 to 1869.

Two officers lived in one of the two officers' quarters: Bvt. Lt. Col. Robert L. Kilpatrick and 1st Lt. Michael J. Hogarty. As in the modern army, the officers' peacetime duties involved routine paperwork and correspondence with regimental and department headquarters. A third officer, 2nd Lt. Douglas Wrigley, was stationed in the South. The troops stationed at the fort during this period were fit only for garrison duty. This photograph shows quarters that were built in 1840. The two outbuildings were used as privies and as storage space for coal and extra furniture.

Commanding officer Bvt. Lt. Col. Robert L. Kilpatrick of Company F, 42nd Infantry, was stationed at Fort Ontario during 1868 and 1869. He and his wife occupied the right side of the officers' quarters.

Michael J. Hogarty, first lieutenant of Company F, 42 United States Infantry, was stationed at Fort Ontario during 1868 and 1869. Hogarty saved records from this time period, and the discovery of his papers made it possible to present this period to visitors at the historic fort today. The New York State Parks and Recreation Department reported that after his service at Fort Ontario, Hogarty moved west, raised a large family, and lived until 1925.

Fort Ontario's role of defending the mouth of the Oswego River eased as the American frontier moved west. The army was concerned with the Indian wars in the West, and life at Fort Ontario took on a routine character. The fort was garrisoned by either a company of infantry or artillery.

This 1870 photograph shows troops in front of the main gate and storehouse. The two small buildings were added after 1867 and were used as offices and guardhouses. Note the main entrance without a gate and the dry moat beyond it.

This aerial view shows Fort Ontario in 1870. By that time the fort included numerous outbuildings and a primary road. The buildings on the west side were stables, and a hospital was located off the road on the east side.

A tower was added to the officers' quarters in 1884, providing a second entrance to the building. The tower was removed in the mid-1960s. This photograph shows some outbuildings remaining from an earlier period and the wooden retaining wall on the bastions. The building on the right was used as a tailor shop, a privy, and for storage.

A porch was added to the front of the officers' quarters, as shown in this photograph. The appearance of the grounds suggests that the photograph was taken sometime between 1905 and 1928, when the fort was not being used.

The garrison at Fort Ontario doubled with the onset of the Spanish-American War in 1898. In September of that year, four companies of the 13th Infantry were transferred to the fort. Since the barracks held only 100 men, the troops encamped on the parade ground. They were trained here and then sent to Cuba. In 1899, 15 soldiers of the 9th Infantry were sent from the fort to the Philippine Islands during the Moro Insurrection. After the Spanish left, the Filipinos expected the Americans to give them their freedom, as had been done with Cuba. The Americans, however, decided to retain control of the Philippines for use as a naval refueling station. Thus, the Filipinos continued fighting for their independence.

Some troops from Fort Ontario were killed in the Moro Insurrection in the Philippines. Other soldiers from the fort served in China during the Boxer uprising, a conflict that was declared to be over on July 4, 1905, but that actually lasted until World War II.

Two men from Fort Ontario earned the Medal of Honor. They were members of the 9th Infantry, sent to the Philippines on March 11, 1899.

Troops at Fort Ontario stage a mock cannon firing in 1899. The officer stands at the rear and the bugler, sergeant, and corporal make up the crew. The gun is from the Civil War and is mounted on the bastion that today is the site of a reproduction cannon at Fort Ontario. It should be noted that all of the buildings had tin roofs during this period.

This 1890s photograph shows members of the 7th Infantry standing in front of the guardhouse. In April 1899, the War Department rescinded its order providing for training at Fort Ontario. Congress cut off money needed to complete improvements at the fort, leaving it outmoded as a defensive installation.

In 1901, the fort was reduced to a caretaker basis. All supplies were transferred to Madison Barracks. The townspeople used the parade grounds as a baseball field. For one year after the army moved out, the fort was guarded by a Sergeant Fawdry, who was plagued by vandals and may have invented ghost stories to scare the youngsters away. This modern-day photograph shows the fort's guardhouse and storeroom.

In 1903, Secretary of War Elihu Root recommended that Fort Ontario be rebuilt as a four-company post. During the next two years, a battalion-sized complex of 24 brick and wood-frame buildings was constructed and the outer works and dry moat were removed. The 23rd Infantry was quartered in the new barracks. This photograph was taken looking up Seventh Street toward the Fort Ontario Military Reservation.

This view shows the parade grounds and the enlisted men's quarters at Fort Ontario. The troops in formation are of the 24th Infantry, 2nd Battalion.

By 1905, a much enlarged military reservation existed at Fort Ontario. Its mission had changed from defense to training. Infantry and later coast artillery units were assigned to the post. New brick buildings were constructed. Meanwhile, the old fort fell into disuse and continued to disintegrate.

During the years before World War I, Fort Ontario had a garrison of between 300 and 400 men. Life at the fort was easy: the soldiers' needs were provided by the government, and their work entailed little hardship. The troops were entertained when film companies used the old fort, pictured here, as a historical background. In 1914, Charles Mack brought a company of 35 to the fort to make a picture. In 1915, actors Pearl White and Lionel Barrymore came with a company to film a movie about the Underground Railroad before the Civil War.

This post-1906 view shows the entrance to Fort Ontario. During this period the fort was not in use. A large garrison existed beyond its walls.

This 1850s view of Oswego Harbor shows the lighthouse with Fort Ontario in the background. Note the wooden walls of the fort, the lighthouse on the far shore, and the light keeper's house next to it. Built in 1822, the house is the oldest home in Oswego. It is currently the residence of the fort's site manager.

Three

Hospital

This photograph dating from 1924 shows troops from the 23rd Infantry in front of officers' quarters No. 1. Note the fort's advanced stage of decay. The rubble on the left is the ruins of an outbuilding that once stood near the enlisted men's barracks.

Troops of the 23rd Infantry pose for a mock execution in front of officers' quarters No. 1 in 1924. No executions occurred at this time. The old fort was abandoned during this period.

This view shows the machine-gun crew of the 23rd Infantry using the old fort for gun practice.

This view shows the entrance to the old fort as it appeared from 1905 to 1928. Note the steamroller in front of the gate and the flagpole mounted on the bastion.

This view shows the enlisted men's quarters before the building was remolded as an officers' club. The small buildings on either side are privies. Note that the porch is enclosed.

This aerial view shows Fort Ontario with its 1905 brick buildings. The fort claimed to be the oldest garrisoned fort in the United States. Some of these buildings can still be seen at the historic site. They were well built and continue to be used after nearly a century.

This 1906 photograph shows the Fourth Street entrance to Fort Ontario. The brick buildings are officers' quarters; the building on left is the commanding officer's home.

With the onset of World War I, the fort's mission changed. After the United States declared war on Germany on April 6, 1917, the War Department decided to use the fort as a medical center and hospital. The facilities were improved, new equipment was installed, and the fort took on the new identity of a base hospital. It was called General Hospital No. 5. The Flower Hospital Unit, Army Medical Corps, garrisoned the post. Medical personal were trained for duty and sent to France. This photograph shows the same scene as the one above, but 11 years later.

This postcard shows General Hospital No. 5 in 1917, the year the first group of 75 medical recruits arrived. Under the direction of a large staff of medical officers, the recruits went through an intensive training course in field hospital work, beginning in July. By August 1917, 400 recruits of the Army Medical Corps had been trained at Fort Ontario.

With Fort Ontario in the background, two sailboats ply the waters of Lake Ontario. The lake has always been ideal for sailing.

This view of Fort Ontario dates from 1917. In front of the fort is the lifesaving station. Although the lifesaving station no longer exists, there is a large Coast Guard station on the east side of the Oswego River.

This wintry view of Fort Ontario was taken on the east side of the Oswego River in the port of Oswego.

The facilities at Fort Ontario soon became overcrowded. The fort was built to accommodate up to 400 men. When the garrison reached 1,000, tents and temporary barracks were erected. Some of the tents are visible in the background of this view, which shows a football game under way on the parade grounds.

This winter scene shows some of the tents set up to accommodate the 1,000-man garrison at Fort Ontario during World War I. Congress appropriated $200,000 for new buildings. The army nurse unit arrived and was housed in a new modern facility, and the 250-bed hospital took in its first patients.

This oblique photograph of Fort Ontario was taken on April 25, 1924. Note the lack of a tent encampment area at the left. The barracks are visible above the parade ground oval. The storehouses are on the right, alongside the railroad track. Oswego is at the top.

Fort Ontario was considered one of the best-equipped hospitals of its kind. After the war, the Veterans Administration authorized the construction of veterans hospitals throughout the county, and the number of patients at Fort Ontario gradually declined. This photograph shows the recreation building, constructed in 1917. The building currently is used by the Oswego Recreation Department.

In 1921, Fort Ontario again became an infantry post. The 28th Infantry was transferred here. These troops from the 28th are at the company building at the main gate of Fort Ontario. The photograph dates from 1922. (Photograph by George A. Reed, author's father.)

The above photograph shows the main gate of the old fort as it appeared in 1922. The earlier view below shows the outer walls and dry moat of the old fort prior to the expansion in 1905. The wooden wall, which was constructed in 1840, and the tower of officers' quarters No. 2, built in 1880, are visible.

The tents in the background of this 1917 photograph suggest that the football players are members of the National Guard.

This 1917 photograph shows a ward at General Hospital No. 5. Troops wounded in the war in Europe were transported to New York City, where they were placed on hospital trains bound for Oswego. The patients were delivered directly to Fort Ontario, where railroad sidings had been constructed. At the hospital they received needed treatment.

This band entertained not only the troops assigned to Fort Ontario but also the patients at General Hospital No. 5.

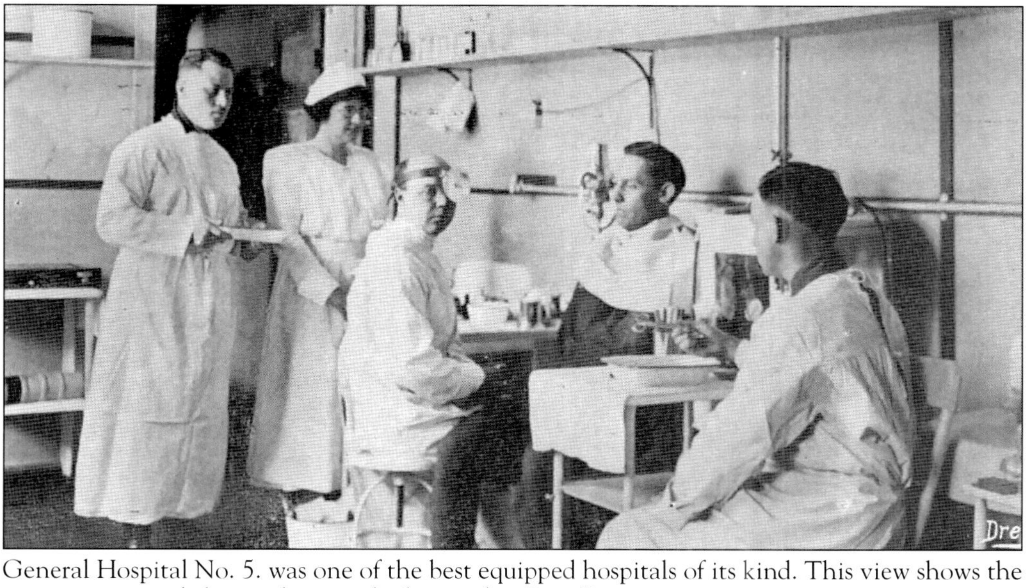

General Hospital No. 5. was one of the best equipped hospitals of its kind. This view shows the eye-ear-nose-and-throat clinic at the hospital at Fort Ontario.

During the winter of 1918, medical troops underwent intensive training at Fort Ontario. Medics and nurses were trained for World War I at what was known as the Flower General Hospital.

This 1918 photograph shows the medical detachment at Fort Ontario. The first 75 Army Medical Corps recruits arrived in July 1917. By August 1917, 400 recruits had received training at the fort.

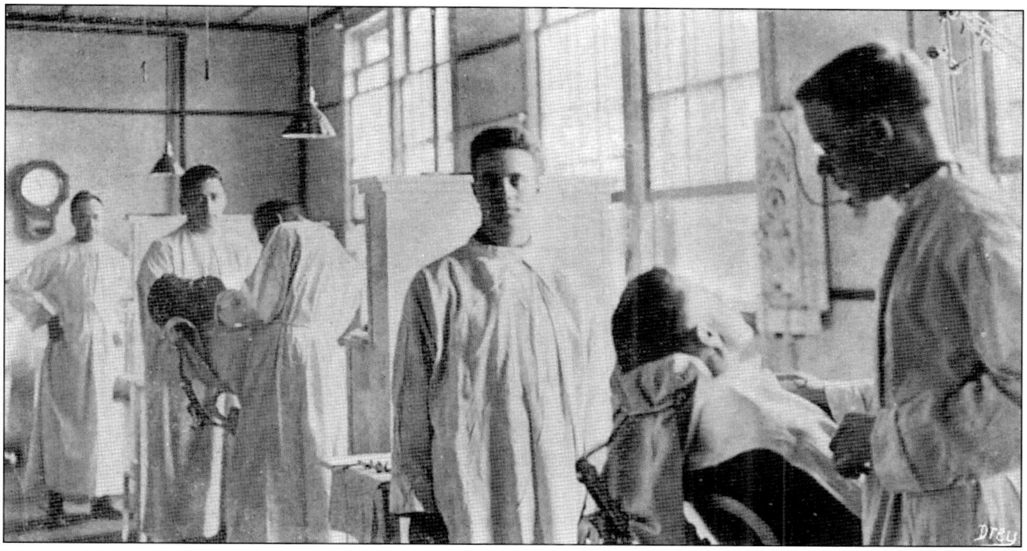

General Hospital No. 5 was a full-service facility. It provided dental care to the army in the dental laboratory shown here.

This 1917 photograph shows one of the hospital wards. Troops that were wounded in Europe were shipped to New York and from there to General Hospital No. 5.

The nurses at General Hospital No.5 were trained right at the hospital. The patients came from the battlefields of France. This view shows some of the hospital's 250 beds.

This is a view of the Red Cross recreation room at Fort Ontario. Shown are troops who were recovering from the wounds they received on the battlefields of France.

Visitors arrive to see patients at General Hospital No. 5. The large building on the right contained recreation facilities. The building in the center left wards for 250 patients.

Capt. A.R. Edward and a staff of 75 men were in charge of the hospital at Fort Ontario.

This photograph shows some of the army nurses at Fort Ontario posing outside General Hospital No. 5.

Four

Last Years as a Fortification

In 1921, Fort Ontario again became an infantry post and remained one for the next 20 years. The 28th Infantry was transferred to the fort. In 1933, Fort Ontario became the headquarters of the army's 1st Brigade. Two battalions of the 28th and Headquarters Company were stationed here. Gen. Charles D. Roberts was transferred from Madison Barracks in 1933. He was succeeded by Gen. Irving J. Phillipson and Gen. Walter T. Short. This view shows the entrance of the old fort as it appeared at the time.

This photograph shows officers' quarters No 1 c. 1920. Note the boarded-up windows and the powder magazine on the right. Prior to Fort Ontario's reactivation as a post, the buildings were boarded up.

This view shows Fort Ontario from the harbor. At the time, the lifesaving station was still in use.

This view taken from Fort Ontario shows ice castles on the Oswego River. These ice formations are created when the river freezes in the winter months.

Junior officers were stationed at Fort Ontario once again. They occupied officers' quarters No. 1, shown here *c.* 1928.

In 1928, the enlisted men's barracks was converted into an officers' club and the old fort took on new life. Other buildings were remodeled into apartments for junior officers. The bastions were developed as a golf course.

The photograph on the left shows a signal corpsman at Fort Ontario in 1927. The photograph on the right shows the sergeant, 1st Brigade, 28th Infantry, at the fort in 1933.

In October 1940, the War Department decided that Fort Ontario would be an ideal site for an antiaircraft artillery unit because of its proximity to Lake Ontario and other natural resources. Each summer, regulars stationed at the post were sent to the Stony Point Rifle Range or Camp Perry in Ohio for special training. National Guard Antiaircraft Regiments from New York, Delaware, and Illinois came here for two-week, summer-training encampments. This photograph shows the National Guard setting up a tent near the walls of the old fort.

Fort Ontario was also selected as a training post for winter maneuvers. Troops were trained in the use of snowshoes and skis. They marched through deep snow and slept outdoors in sleeping bags without shelter. The training proved valuable a few years later in the mountain passes of Italy and the forests of Germany. This photograph shows the 28th Infantry, American European Forces, at Fort Ontario.

Shortly after the passage of the Selective Service Act of 1940, the War Department made a survey of Fort Ontario's facilities in anticipation of using the site as an induction center for new draftees. The post was expanded to provide quarters for a full regiment. More than $1 million

was spent to build 60 new structures. When the work was completed, the post was large enough to hold 3,000 men. By 1941, 125 buildings stood at Fort Ontario.

The above photograph shows the National Guard Antiaircraft Regiment at Fort Ontario. Below, the 369th Coast Artillery was nationalized and called into federal service on January 13, 1941. Organized in 1913 as a "Negro regiment," it was designated as the 15th Infantry. The unit served in World War I and was cited 11 times for bravery. During World War II, the army was segregated by race, although black soldiers had served in all previous American wars. On January 15, 1941, an advance guard of the 369th regiment of the New York Guard consisting of 14 officers and 108 men arrived at Fort Ontario. On January 23, 1941 the balance of the regiment, 1,800 men and equipment, arrived by train. The 369th consisted of two antiaircraft gun battalions and a searchlight battalion. The troops underwent intense training. Day after day, they marched from Oswego to Minetto and then to Fulton or Pine Camp. Antiaircraft equipment was set up on the parade grounds and to the east of the fort. On September 4, 1941, the 369th Regiment was transferred to Camp Edwards in Massachusetts for further training. The 198th Antiaircraft Regiment, part of the Delaware National Guard, was transferred to the fort to replace the 369th. This regiment was enlarged with the arrival of 74 officers and 1,800 men. The governor of Delaware, Walter W. Bacon, visited the fort and inspected the troops.

At the top are officers and troops of the 28th Infantry who were stationed at Fort Ontario in the 1930s. The photograph below shows the National Guard at the fort *c.* the 1920s.

The National Guard sets up summer camp at Fort Ontario in 1920.

The Delaware National Guard was at Fort Ontario when Pearl Harbor was attacked on December 7, 1941. With the outbreak of World War II, the 198th Antiaircraft Regiment was sent to New York City to defend against possible attack. Pfc. Charles Kirby, chaplain's assistant for the 198th, is shown on the left in September 1941. The more recent photograph on the right shows Kirby as a retired warrant officer, holding the insignia of the Delaware National Guard that he removed from Fort Ontario on December 8, 1941.

Five

WORLD WAR II

With the outbreak of World War II, the antiaircraft equipment was transferred to various coastal areas of the United States. German submarines had been spotted off the coast of Long Island, and the War Department felt that the equipment should be closer to possible points of attack. Fort Ontario took on the role of training new recruits as military police. Many of these recruits were well-educated men who had been drafted. The training was brief and after the program was completed, many of the men were sent to various colleges for further educational training in special service activities. The role of Fort Ontario shifted once again, as the 1212th Service Battalion was transferred here. This photograph shows troops from Fort Ontario off duty.

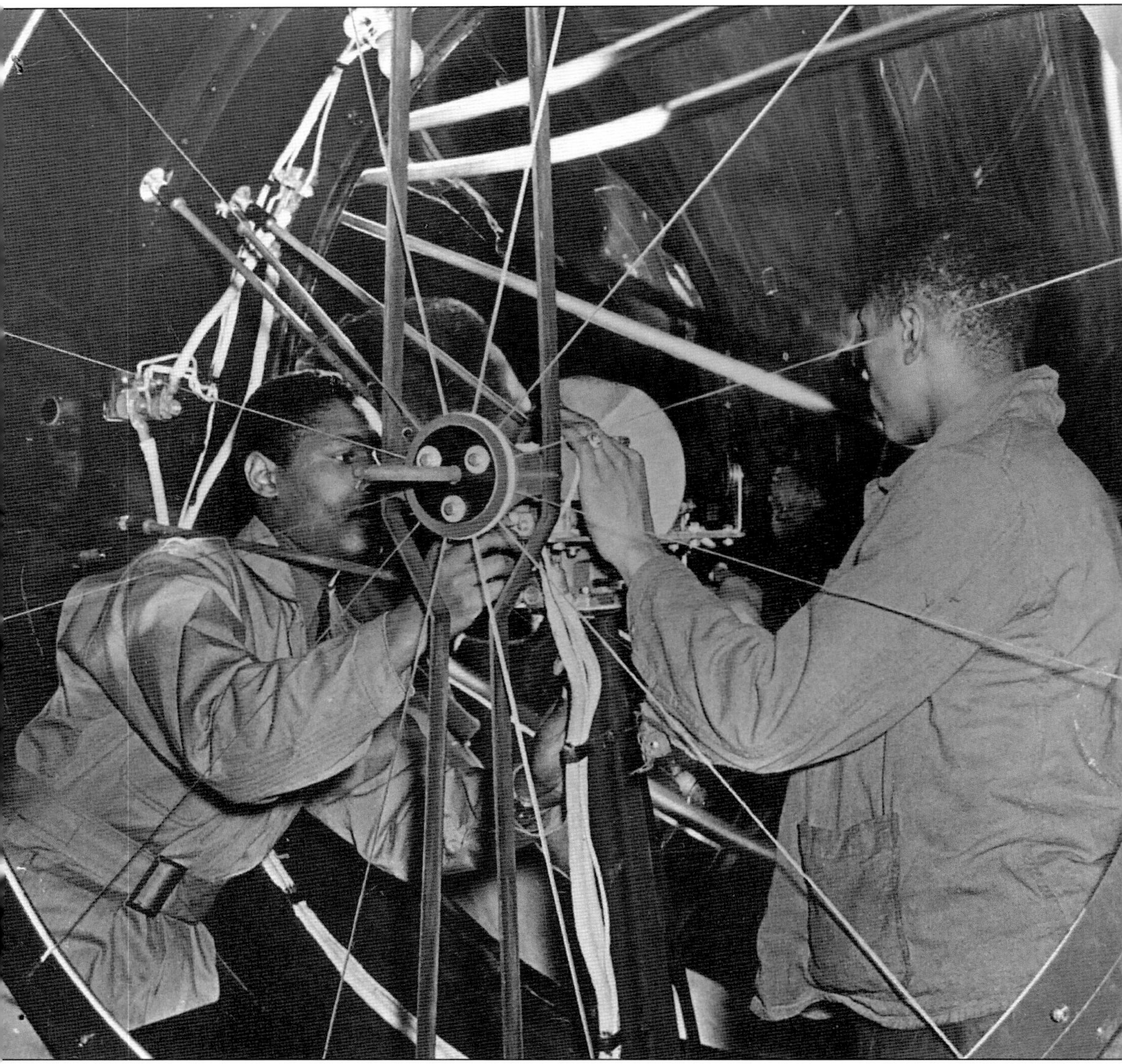

In factories outside the walls of Fort Ontario, men and women worked to produce materials for the war effort. This 1943 photograph shows men working on a large wheellike part at a factory on the west side of Fort Ontario.

United Service Organizations (USO) was located on the second floor of the Knights of Columbus Hall on the west side of First Street in Oswego. To relax after the rigors of training, troops went to the USO for quiet time, socializing, and entertainment. This photograph dates from 1943. The Knights of Columbus Hall burned in 1946.

Many of the men called up under under the Selective Service Act had initially been rejected and given a 4F classification because of illiteracy or having been born in a foreign country. With the onset of the war, however, these men were reconsidered and reclassified. Fort Ontario was chosen as one of two training centers for these men. Professional educators were transferred from other branches of the services to the fort, where they established an elementary level school. The men underwent a six-week program that gave them the equivalence of a fourth-grade education. Troops graduated with the ability to solve simple mathematical problems and to understand and obey specific army orders. Upon completion of training, the men were transferred to various army units. This 1943 photograph shows USO staff and volunteers writing letters home for men in this program who were unable to write them on their own.

The six-week education program was transferred to Pine Camp (Camp Drum) on March 15, 1944. Fort Ontario again became a regular military post. The *c*. 1943 photograph above shows volunteers from Fulton who entertained troops from Fort Ontario at the USO. The photograph below shows some men relaxing in a quiet area of the USO.

The Fort Ontario Orchestra, led by John Mussachio of Oswego, entertained troops at the USO. The band had musicians from some of the big bands in New York.

This photograph shows National Guard troops from the 369th Coast Artillery dancing at the USO in 1941.

Because Oswego had no African-American population, the army transported United Service Organizations women from Syracuse for the 369th Coast Artillery dances at the USO in Oswego. On September 4, 1941, the 369th was transferred to Camp Edwards in Massachusetts for further training.

A variety of entertainment was held at the USO in Oswego. This photograph shows troops enjoying themselves in 1943.

The photograph above shows officers from Fort Ontario and the mayor of Oswego at a Halloween party at the USO in October 1943. The photograph below shows another scene at the same party.

Troops from Fort Ontario were entertained at the homes of Oswego residents active in United Service Organizations. These two photographs show a USO corn roast held at the home of Dave Russell in 1943.

Six

Safe Haven

Between 1944 and 1946, Fort Ontario was used as an emergency center for 982 refugees fleeing the Nazi Holocaust. The fort was the only wartime refugee shelter in the history of the United States. It was operated by the War Relocation Authority, an agency of the United States Department of Interior. Fort Ontario was chosen as the location for the emergency center as a direct result of a letter from the local chamber of commerce requesting that the fort not be closed. Pres. Franklin Delano Roosevelt was reviewing his options for the refugees when the letter arrived at the White House. Under authority of his wartime powers, Roosevelt ordered that the refugees be transported to Fort Ontario. This aerial photograph shows the wooden barracks used to house the refugees during World War II.

Early on the morning of August 1, 1944, the refugees arrived by train at the eastern side of Fort Ontario. Ninety percent of them were Jews who had fled from 19 Nazi-dominated countries. They were brought here from a part of Italy that had been liberated by Americans troops. The army was responsible for transporting them from Europe and had made some preparation for their quarters. However, once they arrived at Fort Ontario, the refugees came under the jurisdiction of the War Relocation Authority, a branch of the Department of the Interior. They were given asylum in America but were held as prisoners in the camp. The camp was called the Fort Ontario Emergency Refugee Shelter in Oswego, New York. Wooden barracks built at the beginning of the war were converted into living quarters for the refugees. The barracks were located behind wire, near the present post cemetery. Living conditions were sparse. Note the tag on the man's coat; it is his only identification.

Each refugee was assigned the equivalent of one adequate but very stark room. Family groups were kept together. A community store was established in the former Army Post Exchange. Food was provided and meals were prepared by the refugees in community kitchens. A maintenance authority, fire department, and police department were set up. During the first month, the refugees were not permitted to leave the fort. After that, they were allowed to leave the fort during certain hours to shop. Eventually, all limitations on visits to Oswego were removed except for an 11:30 p.m. curfew. The refugee children, who numbered more than 200, were entered in Oswego schools. Their parents were taught English in adult education classes. The refugees formed an orchestra and were invited to appear before local groups. Many of the refugees had relatives in other parts of the country whom they were not permitted to visit. Their most pressing concern, however, was what would happen to them after the war. On December 22, 1945, Pres. Harry Truman signed an executive order granting the refugees freedom and the right to apply for immigration status. In February 1946, it was decided that those who wished to do so could legally enter the United States from Canada as immigrants. In April 1946, the last of the refugees left Fort Ontario.

A monument was erected at the site of the wooden buildings that housed the refugees from 1944 to 1946. The monument reads as follows:

From 1944–1946 Fort Ontario
served as a haven for
982 survivors of the
European Holocaust.
Erected October 25, 1951, by
Syracuse Pioneer Women/Na'amat
and the Jewish community
of central New York

At some point, the monument was vandalized and the word "Jewish" was defaced by someone who did not wish to remember the past.

Seven

HISTORIC SITE

At noon on April 3, 1946, Fort Ontario ceased to be a military institution. Having outlived its usefulness, the fort was declared surplus and was placed under the jurisdiction of the New York State Housing Commission. As the flag was lowered from the 50-foot pole at the northwestern corner of the parade grounds, Col. J.M. England of the 9th Army-Air Force said, "Thus, Fort Ontario ceases to be part of the United States Army." The last load of military equipment was taken from the fort through the East Seventy Street gate. Twenty-five civilian employees remained on duty until midnight. Immediately, there was interest in developing the fort as a historic site. However, because of the old fort's dilapidated condition, that transfer was delayed until 1949. During 1946, most of the wood-frame structures were torn down in preparation for conversion of the brick buildings into veterans housing units, which were to be leased to the City of Oswego for five years.

Oswego Mayor John Scanlon, right, welcomes a British officer, Lady Harthwicken, and a Polish air force officer to a United Nations program held at Fort Ontario in 1946, above. After Pres. Franklin Roosevelt proclaimed United Nations Day, Scanlon announced United Nations Week and invited fighting men of America's Allies to come to Oswego and to local homes. The photograph below shows a Boy Scout picnic held at the home of the president of Oswego State Teachers College for United Nations work at Sheldons Point.

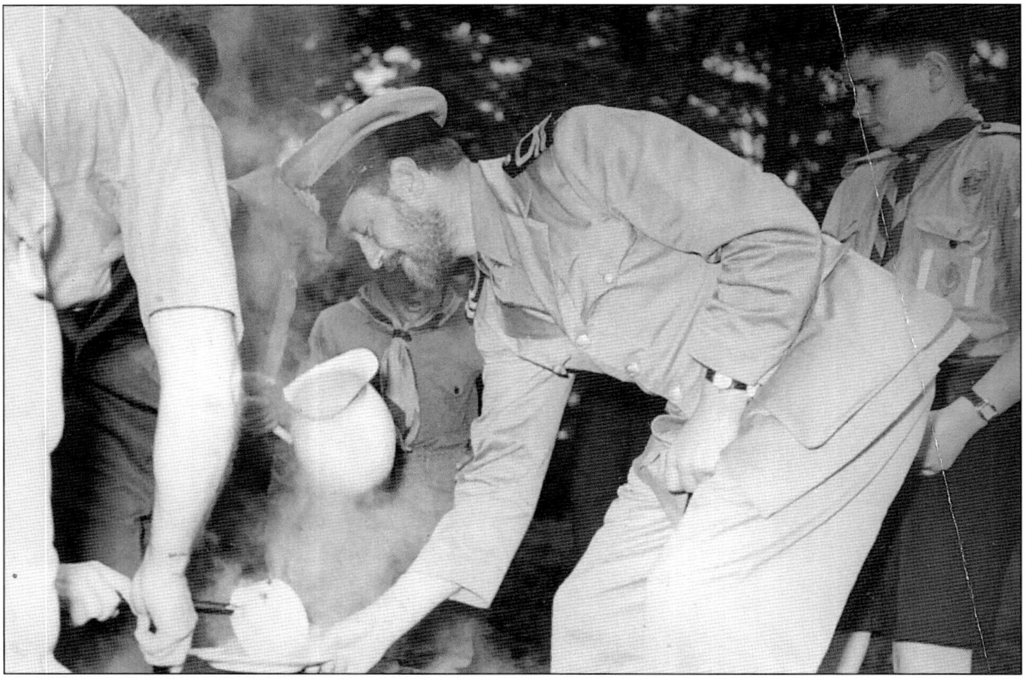

Visitors here for the United Nations program in 1946 prepare to depart, above. The train station is now Pauls Big M Market. Below, visiting servicemen board a train in Oswego to return to their units at the end of United Nations Week.

Troops from Poland, Denmark, France, and New Zealand visited Oswego during United Nations Week in 1946. This photograph shows some of them departing after the celebration.

In 1947 and 1948, historians from the state museum visited Oswego to further investigate the possibility of making the fort a state historical site. Renovations were undertaken by the New York State Department of Education. Finally, in 1949, Fort Ontario became a state historic site. The transferred site was smaller than the military post of World War II. The City of Oswego retained many of the older brick buildings and used the parade grounds for sporting events. In 1962, fort curator Wallace Workmaster and the Oswego County Junior Chamber of Commerce developed the Fort Ontario Guard, shown here. Workmaster proposed "engaging a group of young men who would be drilled in the military routine of 1860, . . . dressed in the precise uniform of the period, and used at the fort to mount the guard. [They would] present dress drills and otherwise help to establish the climate of history which is so important to a restoration of this kind."

Historian Rosemary Nesbitt, left, participates in an archaeological dig held at Fort Ontario in 1965, above. The photograph below shows one of objects found on the site in 1965: a button from a uniform of the 49th Regiment, which served during the days of the French and Indian War.

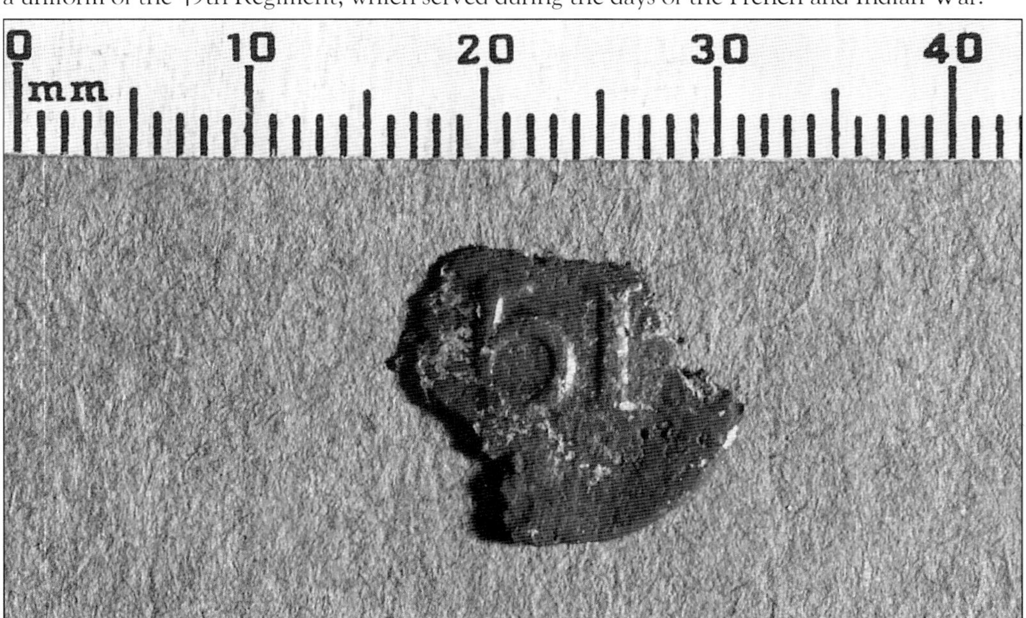

The winter scene above, dating from 1965, shows rifle casemates at the west wall of Fort Ontario. The photograph below shows the road that circled the old fort prior to renovations undertaken in 1968. The road, the benches, and the trees were all removed in 1968.

The historic site offered tours for groups both old and young, such as these children, photographed as they march up to the main gate of Fort Ontario. Visitors who came during the July 1-to-Labor Day period got to see the Fort Ontario Guard on duty daily from 9 a.m. to 5 p.m. and Sundays from 1 to 5 p.m.

Although the drill of the Fort Ontario Guard was based on military manuals from the Civil War period, much of it reflected military training from the 1960s; the military experience and training of some early guard members and leaders was incorporated into the drill. A major influence on the Fort Ontario Guard was visits made to Fort Henry in Kingston.

Uniforms for the Fort Ontario Guard were originally purchased from Saxony Clothes and Uniforms in New York City. The first ones were made of polyester; later ones were made of wool, but the style remained the same until 1985. Each member was equipped with two uniforms: an infantry uniform for daily use and an artillery uniform for dress occasions. Footwear consisted of Wellington boots. Lieutenants wore a double-breasted staff officer's uniform. Over the years, the size of the Fort Ontario Guard grew and contracted as budgets fluctuated. However, little else changed. From the 1960s to the mid-1980s drills, uniforms, and arms remained the same. The guard was armed with reproduction muzzle-loading rifles, purchased from Norm Flayderman in Greenwich, Connecticut.

The Fort Ontario Guard was, in fact, a generic army unit that presented programs on the life of a soldier at the fort. The mixture of pre- and post-Civil War uniforms, weapons, and drill manuals created a unit that never existed. This c. 1965 photograph shows the powder magazine with a member of the Fort Ontario Guard on duty.

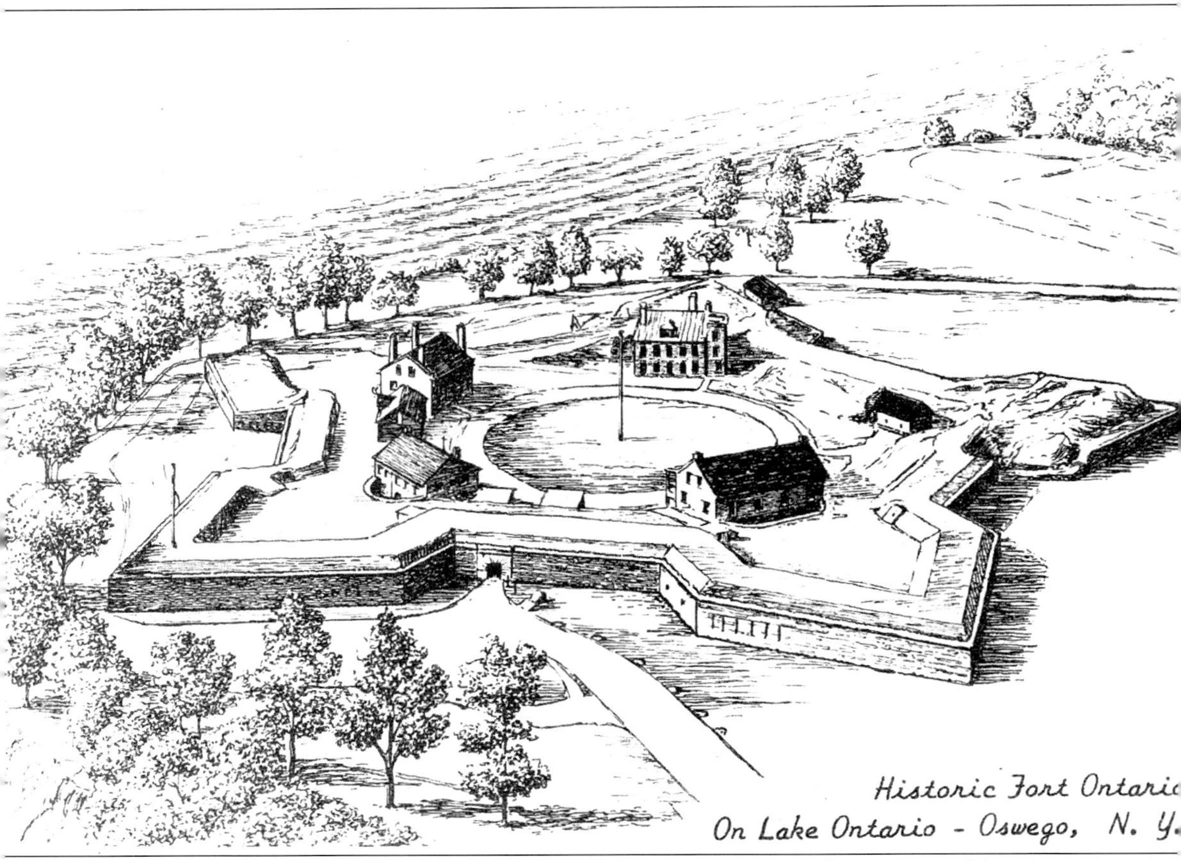

This pen-and-ink drawing was used in advertisements and literature that promoted Fort Ontario. The drawing was done prior to 1968.

The photograph on the right shows the restoration crew removing the wall in the tower of officers' quarters No 1 in 1968. The old fort was laboriously reconstructed to a hypothetical image of its appearance after the Civil War, below. Cement walks were replaced by brick paths. Tin roofs were replaced by wood shingles. Building interiors were restored according to their 1839 blueprints.

A museum was opened on the second floor of the enlisted men's barracks. Its display covered the entire history of Fort Ontario. The museum is no longer open to the public.

Some mistakes were made during the restoration of Fort Ontario. The buildings were furnished with items dating from 1820 to 1900. Some of the furniture came from the Kingsfords, a wealthy mercantile family from Oswego. The wallpaper shown here was a copy of a French design. The image of wealth presented in the officers' quarters was not typical of the furnishings used during the fort's active years. In 1985, a project was undertaken to redo the interiors to better reflect the period from 1867 to 1872.

State historian Albert B. Corey located two Civil War cannons for Fort Ontario at Washington's Headquarters in Newburgh. The cannons arrived at the fort in May 1955, but no gun carriages were available. The Corrections Department at Lorton, Virginia, was unable to provide them because it was authorized to do work for only the federal government or the District of Columbia. No commercial firms made carriages in 1955. It virtually took an act of Congress for Fort Ontario to acquire its gun carriages: Congressman Leo O'Brien prepared the bill that eventually enabled the New York State Education Department to buy gun carriages from Lorton. On February 3, 1958, the carriages were shipped to Fort Ontario, and the cannons were mounted on June 12, 1958.

This rose-and-crown cannon was found in the St. Lawrence River. Mounted on a reproduction carriage, it was given to Fort Ontario. Records suggest that the cannon was once at Fort Ontario. The gun is currently on loan to Canada.

This 1970 photograph shows the interior of Fort Ontario. Note the brick sidewalks and the stone walls; both are historically incorrect: the sidewalks should have been slate, and the wall should have been a log structure. In addition, most of the roofs should have been tin and the powder magazine roof should have been slate.

These photographs show the Fort Ontario Guard drilling and parading in front of spectators in the 1970s. The guard's performances were designed to entertain visitors.

This photograph shows the U.S. Marine Corps color party at Fort Ontario in 1980. The marines visited the old fort many times over the years. The early Fort Ontario Guard modeled its drill on that of the Marine Corps.

The Brigade of the American Revolution made frequent visits to Fort Ontario. The brigade is shown here in full uniform, which includes dark blue coats and facings of either red, white, or beige, depending on the unit.

Site manager Wallace Workmaster, center, discusses the Fort Ontario Guard with Ken White, the guard's first lieutenant, and Richard Camp, the guard's first sergeant. The military detachment made its first appearance in June 1962. The guard itself became history in 1985 when, after 23 years, it changed its role and became the 42nd Infantry Regiment, Veterans Reserve Corps, with new dress and equipment. The artillery fired by the 42nd were never used at Fort Ontario in the years 1868 to 1869.

The photograph on the right shows Oswego city historian and author Rosemary Nesbitt standing next to a monument dedicated to hearth and home, the role of women in American history. The scene below shows her at a grave at the Fort Ontario Post Cemetery. The military cemetery was transferred along with the fort as part of the Fort Ontario State Historic Site.

In 1841, this house outside the walls of Fort Ontario was transferred to the War Department, which used it first as a post hospital and later as officers' quarters. Today, the house is one of the oldest buildings still standing in the city of Oswego. Built c. 1821 by the U.S. Treasury Department for the keeper of the Oswego Lighthouse, it is a rare example of a central-chimney house, more commonly built in the days before the mid-18th century when central hallways became popular.

Native Americans, Dutch and English fur traders, the British, the French, American soldiers, Irish immigrants, African-Americans, and Jewish refugees all were a part of Fort Ontario's long history. The site has been designated as the longest continuously garrisoned post in the United States. The men and women who served and died to defend it deserve the respect they earned. The post cemetery marks the graves of troops from Fort Ontario who died in service to their country. Infants and family members were also interred at the site. The sign over the cemetery gate, shown below, has since been removed.

This photograph shows the gravestone of Fort Ontario's reputed ghost, George Fikes. Fikes was either a corporal or a sergeant who served and died at Fort Ontario. In later years, his stone was moved for safekeeping. Ghost stories were created by caretakers to frighten children away from the fort. As time went on, the stories grew. In 1999, workers claim to have seen large groups of ghosts at the historic site.

Eight

Recent Years

Although Fort Ontario has undergone many changes since it was transferred to the New York State Parks and Recreation Department in 1973, the historic site has yet to reach its full potential. Working with few resources, a very small staff has heroically tried to maintain the crumbling structures. Here, Richard LaCrosse, left, is shown inspecting the walls of Fort Ontario, accompanied by Allan Oullette. Rifle casemates are visible in the foreground.

In 1989, a smooth-bore reproduction cannon was mounted at the historic site to represent the 12 guns that once defended Fort Ontario. It is a non-firing cannon.

In 1985, the 42nd Infantry Regiment, Veterans Reserve Corps, replaced the Fort Ontario Guard. The new unit depicted a company of Civil War veterans, many of whom were disabled by war wounds. The above photograph, taken in 1993, shows the corps reenacting Battery A, 3rd U.S. Artillery. The photograph below shows a crowd of people who are waiting to see the battle of the tall ships during Harborfest in 1993.

The 42nd Infantry Regiment, Veterans Reserve Corps, prepares to fire its cannon in 1999. The crew loads and primes the gun under the watchful eye of George Reed, dressed as a *c.* 1867 captain of engineers.

The 42nd Infantry Regiment, Veterans Reserve Corps, recoils as the cannon fires. Below, members of the 42nd fold the garrison flag at the end of the day.

The 148th New York Volunteer Infantry, above, poses with the Veterans Reserve Corps at Fort Ontario in May 1999. Below, the 148th fires a volley. Visible in the background of this May 1999 photograph is the site manager's home.

A flag ceremony, right, is held on the southwest bastion at Fort Ontario in 1999. Below, the flag is folded in the correct manner.

The 148th New York Volunteer Infantry, above, fires a volley from the rifle casemate on the southeast side of Fort Ontario in May 1999. The photograph below shows the outer walls and main gate and a historic 36-star flag. The outer works are gone, and the gun ports are silent.

These two photographs show the officers' quarters at Fort Ontario State Historic Site as it appeared in 1999. The building was constructed between 1842 and 1844. After Fort Ontario was transferred from the New York State Educational Department to the State Parks and Recreation Department, a project was undertaken to restore the building to better reflect the period from 1867 to 1872. Research materials at the National Archives and two watercolors of the interior were used as guides.

The above photograph shows the enlisted men's barracks at the Fort Ontario State Historic Site. Below is the storehouse, which was also used as headquarters. Both photographs were taken in May 1999.

Reenactors pose outside officers' quarters No. 2, above. The view below shows the walls of the fort and the ordinance rifle and garrison gun on the southwest bastion. The gun ports of the casemates are also visible.

Here are two views of Fort Ontario's storehouse, with the guardhouse over the main gate. The lower one shows a reenactor looking over main gate. Both photographs were taken in the spring of 1999.

The above photograph shows the entrance to the southwest casemate, with a view of the officers' quarters. Below, the view from the east curtain wall shows the side of the enlisted men's barracks. Both photographs were taken in 1999.

A school for clerks was held at Fort Ontario by the 148th New York Volunteer Infantry in May 1999. Members of the 148th attended to practice the skills used by clerks during the Civil War years. This photograph shows the clerks learning skills during the morning class.

Col. Jeff Fortais, the commanding officer of the 148th New York Volunteer Infantry, and some of the reenactors find the shade at Fort Ontario in May 1999. Reenactors put on demonstrations of life in Civil War times.

Capt. George Reed and army musician Dave Brown exchange some military history across a Fort Ontario fence.

Two youths choose a pleasant place to sit at Fort Ontario. The boys are sons of members of the 148th New York Volunteer Infantry who are participating at the historic site because they love history. Their parents have provided them with uniforms.

APPENDIX
UNITS AT FORT ONTARIO

1755-56 50th Regiment of Foot
51st Regiment of Foot
Jersey Blues
Royal Artillery

1756 Regiment L' Infanterie Bearn
Regiment L' Infanterie La Sarre
[French Attacking force]
Regiment L' Infanterie Guyenne
Corps of Engineers
Corps Royal d'Artillerie
Compagnies Franches de la Marine

1758 Independent Companies of New York
(Oglevie's & Gates)
Westchester County Militia
(Ogden's Company)
New York Militia (Dobois company)
Dutchess County Militia
(Bladgely's & Humphrey's Companies)
Queens County Militia (Wrights Hewlet's companies)
Suffolk County Militia (Hand's company)
Richmond County Militia (Arrowsmith's company)
Ulster County Militia
(Seeley's & Clinton's companies)
Albany County Militia
(Yates's & Van Schaik's companies)
Boston Militia (William's company)
Massachusetts Bay Militia (Doty's company)
Rhode Island Provincials
New Jersey Provincials
Royal Artillery
Roger's Rangers
Batteaux Men

1759 44th Regiment of Foot
46th Regiment of Foot
60 Regiment of Foot (4th Battalion)
Royal Artillery
New York Provincials

1760 42nd Royal Highland Regiment
(1st and 2nd Battalions)
44th Regiment of Foot
55th Regiment of Foot
60th Regiment of Foot (4th Battalion)
77th Regiment of Foot (8 companies)
46th Regiment of Foot
80th Regiment of Foot
Roger's Ranger Company (Ogden and Waite)
Royal Artillery (Williams)
New York Provincial Battalions
(LeRoux, Woodhull, & Corse)
New Jersey Provincials
(Lyman, Wooster, Fitcher, Whiting)
Connecticut Provincials
(4 unspecified battalions)

1763-66 55th Regiment of Foot

1768 60th Regiment of Foot (Captain Wharton)

1777 34th Regiment of Foot
8th Regiment of Foot
King's Royal Regiment of New York
(Sir John Johnson's Royal Greens)
Butler's Rangers
Anspach Jaegers (Anspach-Beyreuth)

1779 [American attack]
3rd New York Regiment, Continental Line

1782 34th Regiment of Foot
King's Royal Regiment of New York

1796 Detachment of U.S. Artilleries and Engineers

1808 6th Infantry Regiment, N.Y.S. Militia

1813 16th Infantry Regiment, N.Y.S. Militia
22nd Infantry Regiment, N.Y.S. Militia
23rd Infantry Regiment, N.Y.S. Militia
New York State Militia (Onondaga County)

1814 3rd U.S. Artillery Regiment
(Boyle, McIntire, Pierce, and Ansart, Company Commanders)
U.S. Navy Detachment
Royal Navy Detachment
[British attacking force]
Royal Marines
Glengarry Light Infantry Fencibles
Regiment de Watteville

1838 Company A, 8th U.S. Infantry
Company E, 8th U.S. Infantry
Company G, 8th U.S. Infantry

1839 Company G, 8th U.S. Infantry

1841 Battery G, 4th U.S. Artillery
Battery C, 4th U.S. Artillery

1843 Company G, 2nd U.S. Infantry

1848 Company F, 4th U.S. Infantry

1852 Battery C, 4th U.S. Artillery

1854 Battery H, 4th U.S. Artillery

1856 Battery E, 2nd U.S. Artillery

1861 Companies C and D, 2nd Battalion, 16th U.S. Infantry

1862 147th New York Volunteer Infantry
21st Independent Battery of Light Artillery

1863 48th Regiment, New York State Militia
Invalid Corps (August-September)

1864 Company H, 3rd Battalion, 16th United States Infantry

1865 16th U.S. Infantry
Company E, 4th U.S. Infantry

VOLUNTEER UNITS PROCESSED AT FORT ONTARIO

1861 1st New York Light Artillery
81st New York Volunteer Infantry
1862 110th New York Volunteer Infantry
147th New York Volunteer Infantry
21st Independent Battery of Light Artillery

1864 184th New York Volunteer Infantry

1867 Company D, 42nd U.S. Infantry

1868 Company F, 42nd U.S. Infantry
Veteran Reserve Corps

1869 Battery A, 3rd U.S. Artillery

1872 Battery F, 3rd U.S. Artillery

1878 Battery I, 2nd Untied States Artillery
10th U.S. Infantry

1884 Company H, 12th U.S. Infantry
Company D, 12th U.S. Infantry

1881 Battery I, 2nd U.S. Artillery
Battery B, 3rd U.S. Artillery
Company F, 12th U.S. Infantry

1887 Company C, 11th U.S. Infantry
Company C, 6th U.S. Infantry

1892 Company A, 9th U.S. Infantry

1893 Company G, 9th U.S. Infantry

1898 Company C, 9th U.S. Infantry
4 Companies of the 13th U.S. Infantry Trained for service in Cuba (September)

1899 Company I, 7th U.S. Infantry

1900 Company G, 15th U.S. Infantry

1905 23rd U.S. Infantry

1908 2nd Battalion, 24th U.S. Infantry

1917 Flower Hospital Unit, U.S. Army Medical Corps

1921 8th U.S. Infantry

1933 1st Brigade, 28th U.S. Infantry

1941 369th Regiment, New York National Guard
198th Antiaircraft Regiment

1941-44 1210 SCSU
1212th Service Unit
Quartermaster's Corps

NEW YORK STATE EDUCATION AND DEPARTMENT PARKS AND RECREATION

1962-85 Fort Ontario Guard (FOG)

1985- Company F, 42nd U.S. Infantry
Veteran Reserve Corps (Restored)